Symbols, Landmarks, and Monuments

# *Air Force One*

Tamara L. Britton

**ABDO Publishing Company**

# visit us at
# www.abdopub.com

Published by ABDO Publishing Company, 4940 Viking Drive, Edina, Minnesota 55435. Copyright © 2004 by Abdo Consulting Group, Inc. International copyrights reserved in all countries. No part of this book may be reproduced in any form without written permission from the publisher.

Printed in the United States.

Cover Photo: Corbis
Interior Photos: AP/Wide World p. 21; Corbis pp. 1, 4, 5, 6-7, 9, 11, 13, 14, 15, 16, 19, 23, 25, 26, 27, 28; Time Life pp. 12, 18, 29

Series Coordinator: Kristin Van Cleaf
Editors: Kate A. Conley, Stephanie Hedlund
Art Direction & Maps: Neil Klinepier

## Library of Congress Cataloging-in-Publication Data

Britton, Tamara L., 1963-
  Air Force One / Tamara L. Britton.
    p. cm. -- (Symbols, landmarks, and monuments)
  Includes index.
  Summary: Explores the history and usage of aircraft to transport the president, especially Air Force One, the planes which have been a symbol of the United States for fifty years.
  ISBN 1-59197-520-4
  1. Air Force One (Presidential aircraft)--Juvenile literature. 2. Boeing 747 (Jet transports)--Juvenile literature. 3. Presidents--Protection--United States--Juvenile literature. 4. Presidents--Transportation--United States--Juvenile literature. [1. Presidential aircraft. 2. Presidents--Transportation.] I. Title.

TL723.B75 2004
387.7'42'088351--dc22

                                                    2003066004

# Contents

# *Air Force One*

The president of the United States has two airplanes. The crew calls them Special Air Mission (SAM) 28000 and SAM 29000. But when the president boards one of the planes, it becomes Air Force One. This is the **call sign** for any air force aircraft on which the president is a passenger.

Twelve presidents have flown as a part of their job. As **technology** advanced, so did the presidents' planes. Each president's personality affected the planes, both inside and out. History has even been made on board them.

With Air Force One in the background, George W. Bush is greeted with a ceremony in Moscow, Russia.

*Ronald Reagan talks on one of Air Force One's telephones.*

Today, Air Force One is a flying White House. Inside, it contains the latest **technologies** and luxuries. Air Force One has become a symbol of both the presidency and the United States.

# Fast Facts

√ Franklin D. Roosevelt's plane was known as "Project 51" until the press nicknamed it the *Sacred Cow*.

√ A plane called the *Dewdrop* was built for Thomas Dewey when it was predicted he would win the 1948 election. Harry Truman won instead.

√ Lyndon B. Johnson had a leather chair that could be raised and lowered installed at the conference table in Air Force One, facing the presidential advisers.

√ Partway through Richard M. Nixon's flight home after his resignation, Gerald Ford was sworn in as president. At that point, the plane changed its call sign from Air Force One to SAM 27000.

√ Once on board Air Force One, Ronald Reagan would often change into sweatpants so his other clothes would still look nice after the plane landed.

√ A convoy of planes flies with Air Force One. It may include cargo planes with three exact copies of the president's bulletproof limousine, a fuel plane, a press plane, and several others.

√ On a trip to China, the Air Force One convoy carried a bulletproof podium called the "blue goose" for Bill Clinton, as well as a hairdresser for the first lady.

# Timeline

| | | |
|---|---|---|
| <u>1943</u> | √ | On January 11, Franklin D. Roosevelt became the first president to fly while in office. |
| <u>1944</u> | √ | Douglas Aircraft delivered the *Sacred Cow* in June. |
| <u>1947</u> | √ | Harry Truman signed the National Security Act on board the *Sacred Cow*; the *Independence* came into use. |
| <u>1962</u> | √ | SAM 26000 came into service for John F. Kennedy. |
| <u>1963</u> | √ | Lyndon B. Johnson was sworn in as president on Air Force One; the plane flew Kennedy's body back to Washington, D.C., after his assassination. |
| <u>1972</u> | √ | SAM 27000 arrived. |
| <u>1974</u> | √ | SAM 27000 flew Richard M. Nixon home to California after his resignation. |
| <u>1990</u> | √ | SAM 28000 and SAM 29000 came into service. |
| <u>2001</u> | √ | Air Force One acted as a bunker to protect George W. Bush on September 11. |
| <u>2003</u> | √ | Air Force One secretly flew George W. Bush to visit U.S. troops in Baghdad on Thanksgiving Day, making Bush the first U.S. president to visit Iraq. |

# A New Era

The president's job is to run the United States. In the early days of the nation, this was best done from the White House. During that time, travel was slow and difficult. So, the first presidents rarely journeyed far from the central government.

Woodrow Wilson was the first president to visit another country while in office. After **World War I** ended in 1918, he worked with European leaders to make a peace plan. When Wilson went to Europe, he took a ship.

During **World War II** the seas were unsafe. For this reason, President Franklin D. Roosevelt could not travel by ship. Air travel seemed to offer a better chance of arriving safely. So, the **era** of presidential air travel began.

*In the country's early days, presidents often traveled by horse and carriage.*
*Here, President James K. Polk leaves his inauguration in 1845.*

On January 11, 1943, Roosevelt secretly flew to Casablanca, Morocco. There, he met with Britain's Winston Churchill and other **Allied** leaders. Their task was to plan the Allies' European war campaign. For this trip, Roosevelt's plane was a Boeing 314 Clipper. It was called the *Dixie Clipper*.

In 1944, Douglas Aircraft delivered a VC-54C Skymaster for the president. The press nicknamed it the *Sacred Cow*. It had a telephone and an elevator. It also had a room with a seat for Roosevelt, a desk, and a couch for visitors. There was even a bulletproof window so passengers could look outside.

Roosevelt flew only once in the *Sacred Cow*. He traveled to the Yalta Conference in the Ukraine to meet with Winston Churchill and the Soviet Union's Joseph Stalin. Roosevelt died on April 12, 1945, and Harry Truman became president.

Left: *President Roosevelt celebrates his birthday on board the* Dixie Clipper.

Below: *The* Sacred Cow *was used by both Franklin D. Roosevelt and Harry Truman. It was retired in 1961.*

# *Technology Advances*

President Truman flew in the *Sacred Cow* until 1947. That year, a new Douglas DC-6 became the presidential plane. Truman named it *Independence* after his hometown of Independence, Missouri.

The *Independence* was painted to look like an eagle. It had weather radar, autopilot, and could travel 4,400 miles (7,081 km) between fuelings. It could fly nonstop to anywhere in the continental United States.

*Pilot Lieutenant Colonel Henry T. Myers sits in the cockpit of President Truman's plane, the* Independence.

Dwight D. Eisenhower became president in 1953. He had flown in a Lockheed Constellation, or "Connie," while in the military. It was named the *Columbine* for the state flower of Colorado, his wife's home state. Eisenhower wanted the next presidential plane to be a "Connie."

The new plane was a VC-121A Constellation. It was called the *Columbine II.* A picture of a columbine was painted on the plane's nose. The *Columbine II* was the first presidential plane to use the Air Force One **call sign**. Eventually, it was replaced with the Super Constellation *Columbine III.*

# The SAM Planes

John F. Kennedy became president in 1961.  He flew on Eisenhower's backup jets until October 10, 1962, when a new Boeing 707 arrived.  Its **tail number** was 26000.  This was the first official presidential jet.

*SAM 26000 in the final assembly stage at the Boeing plant in Renton, Washington, in 1962*

*John F. Kennedy and his wife, Jacqueline, are greeted in front of Air Force One upon arrival in Dallas, Texas, on November 22, 1963.*

Kennedy had the words *United States of America* added to the plane's body. He also had a picture of the American flag added to each side of the tail.

Kennedy's wife, Jacqueline, was known for her sense of style. So, he encouraged her to decorate the plane's exterior. She hired famous industrial designer Raymond Lowey. He chose the blue, white, and silver color scheme that is still in use today.

When Richard M. Nixon became president in 1969, SAM 26000 was overhauled and remodeled. Nixon gave it the name *Spirit of '76*, in honor of the United States's 200th anniversary. The name was transferred to the next presidential plane when it arrived.

SAM 27000 arrived in 1972. It was very similar to SAM 26000. The old plane became the president's backup. Nixon flew to countries around the world in these planes.

*Richard M. Nixon looks out a window on board Air Force One.*

The next president, Gerald Ford, made good use of Air Force One. He used it to fly both to other countries and within the United States to promote his programs.

Jimmy Carter became president in 1977. He didn't want special treatment. He insisted that Air Force One be a workplace, not a flying palace. He removed the letter *v* from the beginning of the plane's letter and number designation. This was because it meant the passenger was a "very important person."

President Ronald Reagan undid the changes Carter had made. Like the presidents before him, Reagan flew to conferences around the world in Air Force One. He flew to Europe six times, Asia three times, and countries in North America 12 times.

Toward the end of Reagan's presidency, two new planes were ordered. In 1990, the modern 747 wide-body jet SAM 28000 arrived. Boeing delivered **tail number** 29000 later that year.

# Today's Air Force One

Air Force One in flight

Today's Air Force One is actually two planes. They are the SAM 28000 and 29000 planes from 1990. SAM 28000 is the plane the president uses most often. SAM 29000 is the backup plane.

The planes are stored at Andrews Air Force Base in Maryland. There, they are housed in Hangar 19. The U.S. Air Force's Eighty-ninth Airlift Wing takes care of them. These planes can fly anywhere in the world at a moment's notice. Each flight is a military mission.

The planes are secret military **technology**. Some people believe they are equipped with antimissile devices, and a shield that can block an **electromagnetic pulse** resulting from a **nuclear** explosion. But air force officials will not say if this is true, in order to protect the president.

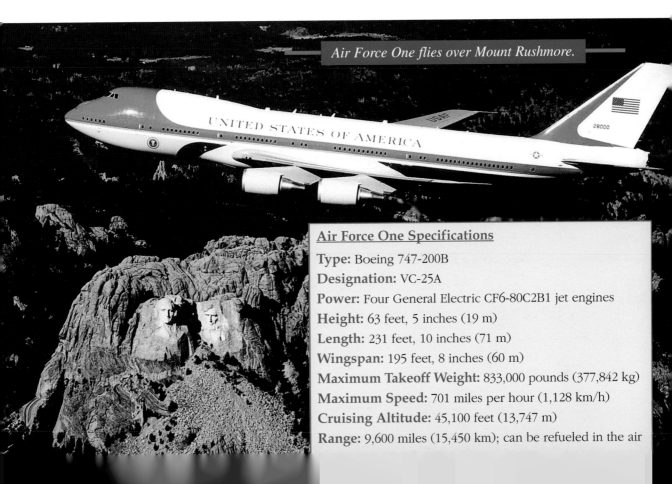

*Air Force One flies over Mount Rushmore.*

**Air Force One Specifications**

**Type:** Boeing 747-200B
**Designation:** VC-25A
**Power:** Four General Electric CF6-80C2B1 jet engines
**Height:** 63 feet, 5 inches (19 m)
**Length:** 231 feet, 10 inches (71 m)
**Wingspan:** 195 feet, 8 inches (60 m)
**Maximum Takeoff Weight:** 833,000 pounds (377,842 kg)
**Maximum Speed:** 701 miles per hour (1,128 km/h)
**Cruising Altitude:** 45,100 feet (13,747 m)
**Range:** 9,600 miles (15,450 km); can be refueled in the air

# Inside Air Force One

The interior of Air Force One is 4,000 square feet (372 sq m). There is room for 76 passengers and a 26-person crew. The passengers can watch movies, television, or use computers. Using the plane's two kitchens, the crew can serve 100 meals per sitting.

Anything the president can do in the Oval Office, he can also do aboard Air Force One. The plane is equipped with 87 telephones. Some are secure. This means the information transmitted through the line is encoded.

The Presidential Airlift Group keeps Air Force One ready for the president's comfort and convenience. The president's quarters include a bedroom, an office, and a private bathroom.

In the conference room are two couches that can be pulled out and made into beds. There is even a **pharmacy** and a medical area on board in case the president gets sick.

On Air Force One, presidents are able to relax. If they wish, they can dress casually and interact with the crew. They can work, read, and watch television without interruption. The controlled environment offers presidents the safety and freedom to just be themselves.

*President George W. Bush talks with Andy Card, his chief of staff. Behind them is a bed that is always made up for the president's use.*

# Security

The White House Military Office plans the president's trips. It works with agencies such as the Secret Service to keep the president safe. Part of this is the strict security around Air Force One.

The presidential planes undergo frequent maintenance. Workers regularly take the planes out for test flights. The engines and tires are replaced often. The crew frequently practices emergency procedures as well.

Air Force One is guarded 24 hours a day. Its fuel is also under guard to prevent tampering. Andrews Air Force Base is surrounded by fences and monitored by high-tech sensors. This keeps people from coming near enough to **sabotage** the planes.

Before takeoff, the runway is checked by hand for debris or damage. Then, the helicopter Marine One brings the president from the White House to Andrews. The president steps on board, and Air Force One takes to the skies.

A police officer guards
Air Force One.

# A Part of History

Air Force One is as much a part of American history as the White House, the Capitol, or the Supreme Court Building. The planes have played an important role in many historic events.

In 1947, President Truman signed the National Security Act aboard the *Sacred Cow.* The act made the U.S. Air Force a separate military branch. It also created both the Department of Defense and the Central Intelligence Agency.

In 1961, Air Force One took President Kennedy to Vienna, Austria. There he had a historic meeting with Soviet **premier** Nikita Khrushchev.

Kennedy was **assassinated** on November 22, 1963, in Dallas, Texas. Just after Kennedy's death, Vice President Lyndon B. Johnson was sworn in as the next president on board Air Force One. The plane then brought Kennedy's body back to Washington, D.C.

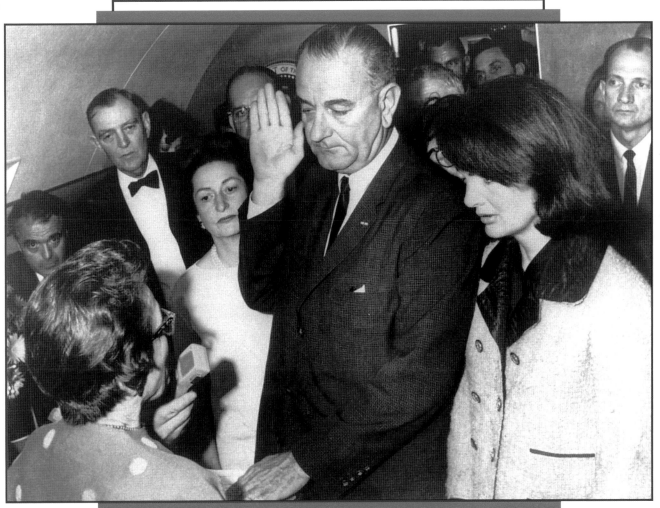

*Lyndon B. Johnson is sworn in as president on board Air Force One just hours after the assassination of John F. Kennedy.*

*President Nixon inspects Chinese troops during his visit to Beijing, China.*

In 1972, President Richard M. Nixon flew on Air Force One to meet with Mao Tse-tung. This made him the first U.S. president to visit China. Air Force One also took Nixon home to California in 1974, after his **resignation** due to the Watergate scandal.

Then on September 11, 2001, President George W. Bush stayed on board Air Force One for the first few hours after the terrorist attacks. The plane acted as an airborne **bunker**. It protected the president until officials knew he could land safely.

Air Force One again made history in 2003. Bush flew in it on a top secret mission to Iraq on Thanksgiving Day. Only a few officials knew about the trip beforehand. Air Force One flew in radio silence with its window shades down so it wouldn't be heard or seen. Once in Iraq, Bush had Thanksgiving dinner with U.S. troops.

*George W. Bush serves Thanksgiving dinner to American troops. Bush was the first U.S. president ever to visit Iraq.*

# America's Plane

Air Force One is more than just an airplane.  It is more than just the president's airplane.  The plane is like an ambassador.  It is the United States in the air.

Americans love Air Force One.  Presidents use this to their advantage.  Air Force One has been the backdrop for many speeches.  President Kennedy would pull right up to the media in the plane.

Air Force One is also a powerful political tool.  The president takes members of Congress on Air Force One to discuss government issues with them.  The excitement of flying on the plane is used to persuade the members to support the president's policies.

Bill Clinton steps off Air Force One at an air force base in Germany.

*Bill and Hillary Clinton are greeted with a ceremony as they step off Air Force One in South Korea.*

Since Franklin D. Roosevelt's first flight, the presidents' planes have flown more than 7 million miles (11,265,408 km). Air Force One is not only a symbol of the presidency, but of the United States as a nation.

# Glossary

**allies** - people or countries that agree to help each other in times of need.  During World War II, Great Britain, France, the United States, and the Soviet Union were called the Allies.

**assassinate** - to murder a very important person, usually for political reasons.

**bunker** - a room or area, often underground, built to keep people safe from attack.

**call sign** - identifying letters, numbers, or names assigned to a person, office, station, or vehicle.  They are used to identify someone in communication, such as by radio.

**electromagnetic pulse** - strong electromagnetic radiation created by a nuclear explosion high above the earth's surface.  It is believed to disrupt electronic systems.

**era** - a period of time or history.

**nuclear** - of or relating to the energy created when atoms are divided or combined.

**pharmacy** - a place where medicines are put together and sold.

**premier** - the highest-ranked member of some governments, also called a prime minister.

**resign** - to officially give up one's job.

**sabotage** - to damage or destroy something on purpose.  Sabotage is often carried out by a person who wants to harm an enemy nation.

**tail number** - an identifying number on the tail of a plane.

**technology** - using scientific knowledge for practical purposes, especially in industry.

**World War I** - from 1914 to 1918, fought in Europe.  Great Britain, France, Russia, the United States, and their allies were on one side.  Germany, Austria-Hungary, and their allies were on the other side.

**World War II** - from 1939 to 1945, fought in Europe, Asia, and Africa.  Great Britain, France, the United States, the Soviet Union, and their allies were on one side.  Germany, Italy, Japan, and their allies were on the other side.

# *Web Sites*

To learn more about Air Force One, visit ABDO Publishing Company on the World Wide Web at **www.abdopub.com**.  Web sites about the president's planes are featured on our Book Links page.  These links are routinely monitored and updated to provide the most current information available.

# *Index*